UNLOCKING
THE CLIENT CODE

How to Continuously Attract Quality Clients

TIMOTHY YOUNG, ESQ.

THRIVING PRACTICES

www.TheThrivingPractices.com

ISBN-13: 978-1541092808

ISBN-10: 1541092805

TABLE OF CONTENTS

TABLE OF CONTENTS

INTRODUCTION

....

ACRES OF DIAMONDS

....

There's a famous story of a man who greatly desired to find vast amounts of diamonds. He lived on a farm and raised animals, making a good living for him and his family, but he longed to be a very wealthy diamond magnet.

One day he decided he wouldn't wait for his dream any longer and he sold his farm and property. He used the money to travel across the world in search of his diamonds, but he was never able to find any. He eventually ran out of money in his search and settled into a job as a common laborer to survive.

Meanwhile, the man who purchased his farm

and property began to explore the land he
had bought. He came upon a small stream
and walked alongside it. As he looked at
the stream, he noticed something glittering
in the sunlight. He went into the stream,
reached down at the glimmering object,
and pulled out a large rough diamond. He
started digging in the stream and found (you
guessed it) acres of diamonds.

All along the restless man's dream of owning
acres of diamonds was right there beneath
his very feet, within his own property. He
was just so fixated on what was happening
elsewhere, that he never found the true value
in all he already had.

Before deciding what's wrong with your
practice and how to change it, first let's start
by recognizing what's great about it. Many
attorneys have no passion at all to grow their

practice. Celebrate that you are taking action and, while you may be frustrated, you want to grow. And that is the most important thing to start any journey.

As you move forward, keep these good aspects of your practice in mind. The simple goal is to do more of what's working and what you like, and less of what's frustrating and devoid of joy.

I JUST NEED TO MARKET MORE

"I just need to market more for new clients..."

At the outset, let me say that I HATE the word 'marketing'. I use it only because it is so ingrained in our business growth vocabulary. To me it sounds 'salesy' and gimmicky, like we're trying to trick the client or consumer with wordplay. Professionals shouldn't have to market. We should offer solid services and have access to clients who need these very specialized services. But we all know it doesn't work that way.

Marketing means a lot of things to a lot of different people. But in the end it's a means to get someone to hire you or buy your product. It's a way of engaging someone else and convincing them that you're the best option for them.

Isn't that simply us communicating with the potential client? If we list our successful verdicts on our website, aren't we simply communicating that information to someone else? And if we run a small ad in the local newspaper explaining the legal services we offer, isn't that basically yet another way of conveying the services we offer?

What if when someone asked you what you were doing for your marketing, you said "I've really started doing some great communicating to my prospective clients... and it's working!" Makes sense right?

Now, if when we 'market' what we are really trying to do is simply communicate to our prospective clients, then that raises a very interesting point:

The reasons you may not have clients knocking down your door is simply because

your communication to them is not working.

If we think of marketing as 'communication',  then instead of saying 'I need to market to get clients…', you should really be saying 'I need to communicate better to get clients'. Wow! Doesn't that have a different feel to it. I challenge you to never again say you have to learn to 'market' better, or that you need to hire someone to help you 'market' your firm. Instead, always use the word "communicate." It has a very different effect on how you feel about your future and how you can grow your practice. Getting more clients isn't some tricky hocus-pocus 'marketing' challenge… it's simply 'communicating' more effectively to your prospective clients.

Now, let's see what, when, where, and how we should be communicating, and, more importantly, who we should be communicating to.

THOSE WHO WANT TO VS. THOSE WHO HAVE TO

Why attracting and 'communicating' with legal clients is different than most others kinds of marketing.

There are at least two types of customers/consumers:

- The ones who are seeking something out because they WANT to.

- Those who are seeking something out because they NEED to but don't want to.

The first thing to realize about legal service clients is that they all fall squarely into the second category. NO ONE *WANTS* to hire a lawyer; they do it only when they feel they need to. You must keep this in mind at all times as you try to communicate to them.

If you're presenting yourself as something they WANT, you will lose. Your communications must be tailored to address their NEED of you, not their WANT of you.

They see you (and your place in their life) as an unwanted need. They believe this entire experience will be *unpleasant* and that it's simply a *necessary evil.*

This seems basic (and maybe you've heard it before), but it's crucial you keep it in mind as you communicate with them. Remember:

1. They don't want to hire you…or any other attorney. They just want their life back.

2. They're mad they're in this situation and, frankly, may view you as one of the

problems.

3. They already think that all lawyers (including YOU) are greedy, untrustworthy and only view them as a way to make money. (And saying you are 'trustworthy' on your website does not change their mind.)

If you consider what drives someone go to a nice restaurant or a 5-star resort, you'll come up with motivators such as: enjoying the experience, relaxing and rejuvenating, sitting by a nice pool with their spouse and reading a great book. Think how far away all of these motivations and goals are from someone who has been badly injured; someone who is scared to death and doesn't even want to hire a lawyer; someone who needs a will but thinks it may cost a fortune and doesn't know why it's so expensive. Or someone up to their eye-balls in debt and who needs to file for bankruptcy, or someone who caught their spouse cheating and needs to get a divorce but dreads the whole process.

Their goal is to not make things worse by hiring an attorney; they don't want to 'look stupid' during the process, and they don't want to be taken advantage of. Frankly, many of the best clients simply don't want to 'feel dirty' during the whole process.

That's a very different viewpoint coming into the relationship with you than someone looking for a nice restaurant or a great resort.

Legal clients are more akin to a cancer patient looking for the best doctor, or a parent searching for a rehab center for a loved one.

Think about your marketing and the

messages you currently say to your perspective clients.

- Are you leading with stories all about yourself?

- Would that appeal to someone who's struggling to fix their own problems?

- What would you want to see on the website of a drug or alcohol rehabilitation center to make you call them? Would it be different than a 5-star resort?

I have been in and out of trial courts for years, and I am reminded of a very fundamental rule of trial strategy: what an injured client says about himself and his suffering is less believable than what others say about him. What we say about ourselves and our practice is automatically scrutinized.

Do you notice the difference between these communications:

Messages attractive to NEED-based consumers

These are messages about where the consumer is now, and how they can move forward and their life will be better:

- You can have a better life and solve your problem.

- Others have been through what you are going through. You are not alone.

- We've helped Joe, John and Bill, who all had the same problem you now have.

- You will get the better life you had before.

- You don't have to figure this out on your own.

Messages attractive to WANT based consumers

Meanwhile, these messages focus on fulfilling hidden desires or stroking one's ego:

- You deserve this thing or experience.

- This thing or experience will make you feel whole.

- You'll feel sexier, smarter, cooler, etc. if you buy this.

- Others will admire you more if you attain this item.

- You will belong to this special group.

These may seem like subtle differences, but when you're the consumer looking for help, saying the right thing can really resonate.

Let me tell you about myself...and more about myself...and more about myself...

Before creating any type of communication for potential clients, decide what voice/tone you're going to use.

- What role will you assume when speaking to your potential clients?

- Will you be commanding them as God from above, like many attorneys do when they speak to clients and others?

- Or will you be subtler and assume the role of a calm guide, coach, or mentor?

There has been a lot written about 'story' and how all humans crave a story. We learn through them and we seek them out. Under the excellent trial advocacy classes taught by David Ball and Don Keenan, an attorney in Atlanta, Ball and Keenan teach that we communicate best with a jury when we put the facts into a story format. Add to this the idea that consumers are really characters in a 'story' (their lives), and we see clearly that the best communications should be related to storytelling.

But how do we do this?

IT'S NOT ABOUT YOU

CHAPTER TWO

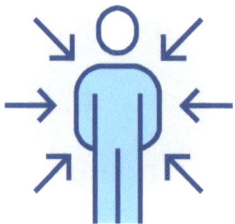 The first realization is that *it's not about YOU!* Your clients want to be the main character in their own stories. They want to be the heroes. They **DON'T** want to be a small part in your exciting story as a wealthy, successful trial attorney.

Do the messages you send to your potential client say "Welcome to my story, here is your small part"? Or are you helping to make their stories (lives) better and more interesting? If a potential client is going through their life and everything is great until all of the sudden they get injured, will they want to join your story of success and money and high dollar verdicts? Not likely.

What if instead they heard you saying things like, "Look, you're worried about medical treatment and here is how we can get it for you…". Or maybe, "you have taken a slight detour from your great story you were living, let's get you back on your track and back into the game."

The 'role' you take when communicating with your potential clients matters a lot.

Think about a successful football team. You and your law firm are not the star quarterback. Guess whose role that is— yep, your potential client. You and your firm play the wise, modest head coach. The quarterback is celebrated. He may even brag a little and show off. People want to *be* the quarterback. The coach is respected. He doesn't brag or showboat. He does state his winning record, but ONLY so other star quarterbacks want to join his team. A coach may say, "I've got some good plays and I can help you win the game as the quarterback." He may even say "I know you have been having a rough streak, but I can coach you back to winning and being a celebrity." He doesn't say "this victory was all about me, and without me, you'd be nothing."

Thinking of your potential clients as celebrity quarterbacks also helps shape how you treat them when they come to your office. You and your office are excited to see them. They are 'celebrities' and they win the games. It's about them and their story, not you or your story.

SPEAKING TO THE ONE, NOT THE MANY

Why an inch wide and mile deep pays a ton more than a mile wide and an inch deep.

Good communication to prospective clients begins by speaking very specifically to them. Think about your everyday life and how businesses communicate with you and which communications you respond best to.

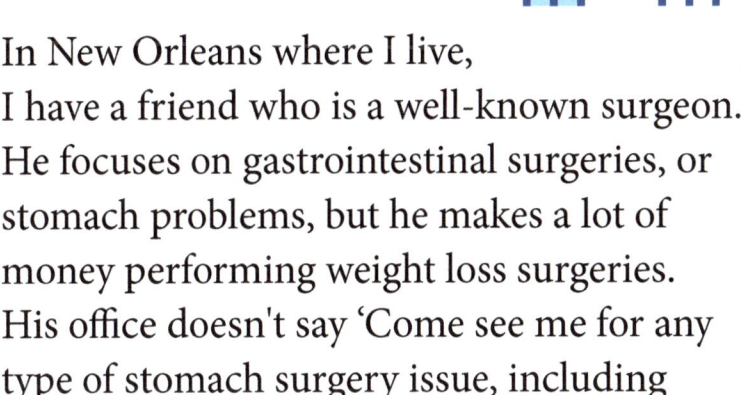

In New Orleans where I live, I have a friend who is a well-known surgeon. He focuses on gastrointestinal surgeries, or stomach problems, but he makes a lot of money performing weight loss surgeries. His office doesn't say 'Come see me for any type of stomach surgery issue, including weight loss surgeries'. Instead, he runs a very specific ad that talks all about the benefits of being slimmer and 'more attractive' and only mentions his stomach surgeries in that ad. In short, the ad speaks directly AND ONLY to females looking for a weight loss stomach surgery. Sure, he does other surgeries and is very qualified to do so, but he doesn't mention any of them in that ad. Why would he?

The more people your communication speaks to, the less effective it will be.

It has to be that way. Why would a general communication appeal to anyone on more than a superficial level? If a local grocery store tells me they sell a lot of everything, I'll think 'gee, that's interesting. Maybe I'll stop by one day'. But if a grocery store tells me they have 9 types of exotic meats and have won 5 awards for the quality of their exotic meats, and the best chefs in New Orleans buy their meats from them, then that's the first place I'm going to get my steaks.

BUT, that same store may also have more than 100 micro-brewery beers in stock, but I can bet you I won't hear about those in that communication about the exotic meats. If they were to mention the large selection of beers they also have, it would send a mixed message to me. I may then start to think, 'gee, maybe the place will be too crowded when I go since it sounds like a warehouse-type place.' Or maybe I associate micro-beers with college kids, and I then start to think 'maybe too many young kids will be there for my taste.'

<u>Every additional bit of information you insert into a communication has some effect on the person reading it.</u> Sometimes it's a good effect, and sometimes it's a bad effect. <u>Words matter.</u> (Please reread this paragraph since it may be the most important information in this book!)

Now think of what most lawyer communications say: "Experienced," "Lots of large settlements," "We handle all injury cases."

Not to be blunt, but what the hell do all those clichés mean, for example, to an uninsured/ under-insured, motorcycle guy crippled by a drunk driver who was borrowing the car from a friend?

What if, instead, we said something like:

"Despite being hit by a drunk driver, our client Jim was able to pay his medical bills and recover money from the owner of the car as well as from his own insurance company. This let him pay his bills and keep his house while he was out of work and recovering over 6 months. Learn how we helped him do all this by calling us now."

Ahhhh… but here is where you say 'but how many 'Jims' are out there, and won't that communication only attract people just like 'Jim'?' This is simply an example to show you how to speak directly to someone like Jim. You can certainly 'pull it back' a little and make it slightly more general. Maybe you drop the drunk driver and make it simply 'a driver'. Or you leave out the part about the borrowed car. The point is all of this gets you thinking from your client's perspective.

The success of your communication is directly related to a three simple things: Market Size (MS), Communication Specificity (CS), and Message Uniqueness (MU).

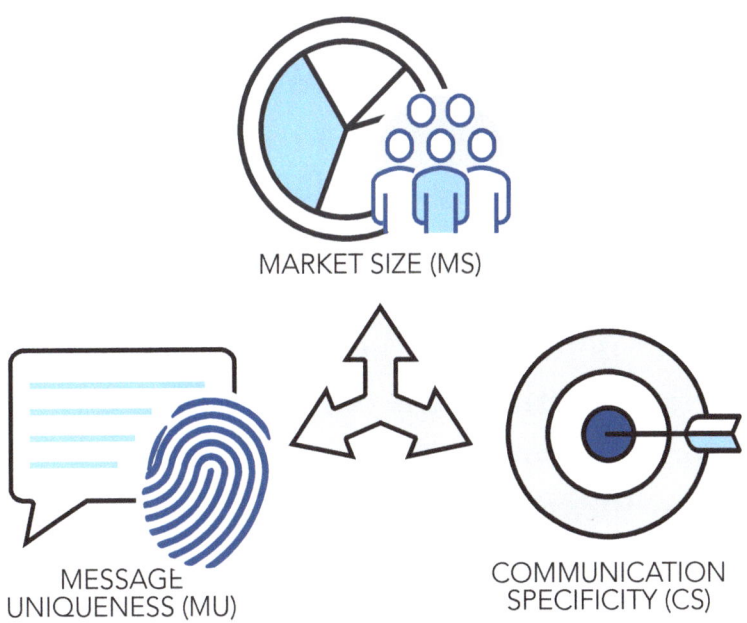

MARKET SIZE (MS)

MESSAGE UNIQUENESS (MU)

COMMUNICATION SPECIFICITY (CS)

1. **Market Size (MS):** the number of people in your market that the communication applies to. In other words, if you say 'we only represent women', then how many women are in your market?

2. **Communication Specificity (CS):** How specific is the communication. Are you saying "hey, men who are over 60, with diabetes and who have suffered an eye related illness after taking a medication," or are you saying "hey, anyone that's injured in any way."

3. **Message Uniqueness (MU):** Finally, the elephant in the room, and why MOST LAWYER COMMUNICATIONS DON'T WORK: how many other people are saying the same or a very similar communication? The more people saying the same thing, the more that your prospective clients will group you all together and then decide who to contact based on some random factor that you have no control over (which is scary since

it means the success of your business is not in your own hands!)

A good formula on the likely success of your communication is simply:

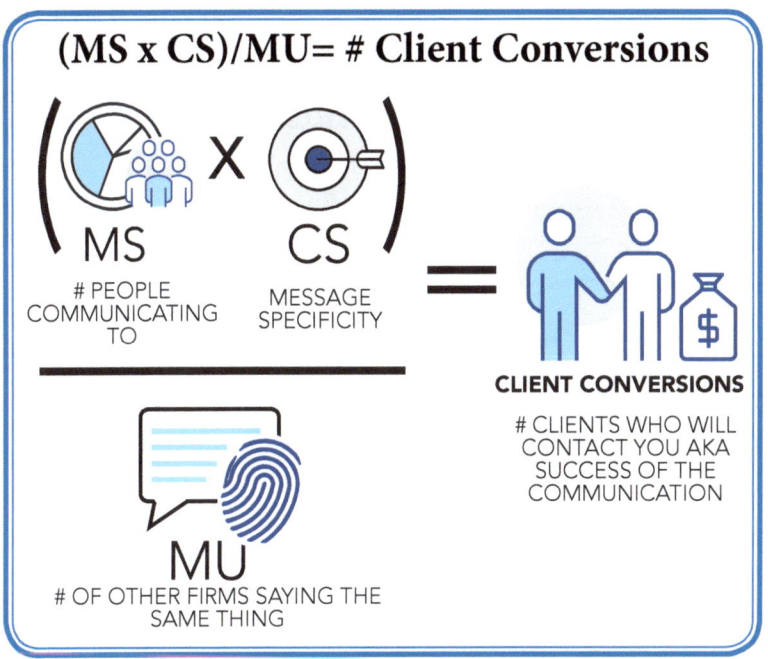

So, what does this formula mean when you go to craft a communication for prospective clients? Simple. You identify a type of client, then simply follow the factors.

Let's say you want to attract injured motorcycle riders and you practice in

Phoenix. You start with a basic message of *"Injured while riding a motorcycle? Call me."* Under our formula, we can see that…

MARKET SIZE (MS)

MS = Phoenix, which has lots of motorcycle riders! That's good news so far.

COMMUNICATION SPECIFICITY (CS)

CS = Not so good here. All we say is for *any* motorcycle rider to call us…hummm

MESSAGE UNIQUENESS (MU)

MU = Oops…big problem. LOTS of lawyers in Phoenix say the same thing They all want these cases.

CLIENT CONVERSIONS

# of clients who will contact you = probably not a lot.

They're hearing the same thing from lots of other lawyers and they will decide based on some random factor you can't control.

But what if we tweak the communication a little bit?

Instead of saying "Injured while riding a motorcycle?" we say *"Are you 30 to 45 years old and have been injured while riding a motorcycle?"*

Look what we just did. We know that 30-45 year olds usually have high loss of future wage claims since they are younger. So, we have an added bonus of only speaking to the better clients for us. But we also made the communication a lot more specific. Granted, we have decreased the size of the market that we're speaking to, but remember that we may not have lost a lot by doing so since we have now better defined the more valuable market.

This all sounds so simple and easy to understand, yet attorneys always fall victim to the Market Size (MS) and insist that they must speak in generalities to everyone, which means they're saying nothing to anyone in particular. The larger the market size, the more you should drill down and be more specific with your communication. And you should always consider how many other people are saying the same thing you are saying (the MU), since this directly dilutes your message and reduces the success of the communication.

If you think this formula is all a bunch of hype, then think of it a different way.

Let's say all ethical rules against direct solicitation of injured clients were erased.

You hear about a fellow down the block who got hurt at work and had his arm amputated by malfunctioning machinery. You know from your other cases that this machinery has had similar problems. You go over to visit him and talk to him about his situation. You're now in front of a MS of one. The market size is a single, specific person.

Next, what are you going to say? Will you communicate that you handle injury cases and are 'experienced' and 'aggressive'? Or are you going to say that (1) you have handled six other cases involving amputations and you know the issues and medical problems that he may have in the future, and (2) you have three other claims against the same machinery manufacturer.

And let's add in the last factor— how many other lawyers will communicate the same message to him? If you say you're experienced and handle injury claims, probably a lot. If you communicate the other message to him, not many (if any at all) will communicate the same thing.

You may be saying, "OK but that's different. That's if I'm in front of a single person…and of course I would know how to communicate to him."

BUT WHY THE HECK WOULD YOU COMMUNICATE ANY DIFFERENTLY TO LOTS OF PEOPLE? People are people. The same rules apply when 100 people view your message as if one person alone views it. Those 100 people are just one hundred separate, single people. This is a foundational rule you must accept if you want to effectively communicate to prospective clients.

- What communications are you now making to your prospective clients?

- How do those communications fare under the formula above?

- Can you see direct, specific ways to make those messages better by changing the market size or the communication specificity, both of which will increase the message uniqueness?

MARKETING TRIANGLE

CHAPTER FOUR

Dan Kennedy (an incredible marketer, copywriter, business developer, and consultant who I highly recommend) has the basic idea that there is a marketing triangle. This triangle includes the market, the message and the media.

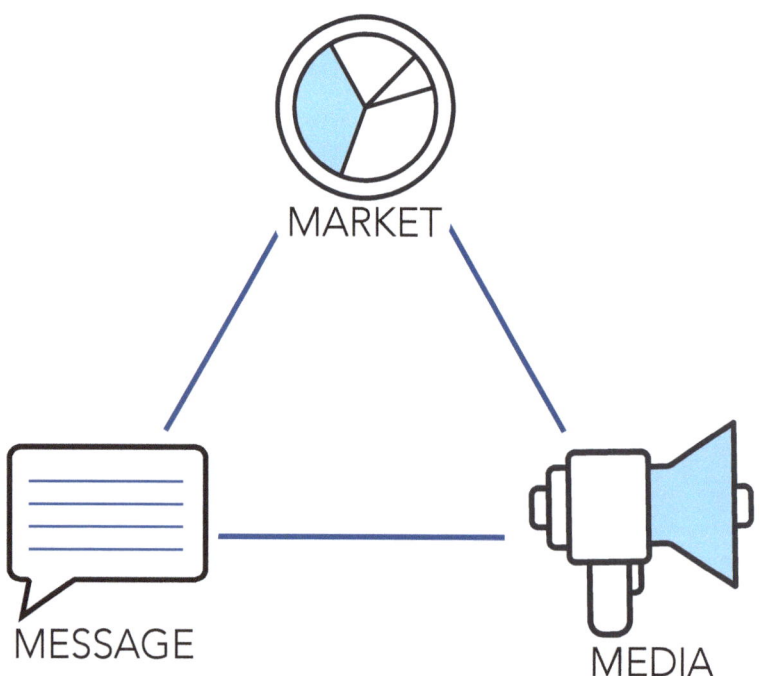

The Market

The market is "who" you're talking to. If you run a television ad in New York on primetime TV, you're speaking to a huge market made up of men, women, children, from a variety of ethnic backgrounds. Basically, your market is "any human" in that geographic area that watches primetime TV. On the other hand, if you place a small print ad on a bulletin board in a college dorm, your market is only those students that would walk past that board. Simple concept, but very important to understand as you pick and choose your market.

The Message

The message is "what" you're conveying. It's the words, colors and images you use in your communications. It's headlines like "Big sale next week…50% off," "Buy one, get one free," or "Hurt in a car wreck? Talk to me!"

The Media

Finally, the media is the means that you use to communicate, or "how" you communicate. These can be traditional ways like billboards, TV, magazines, online and radio. But also more specific and niched ways such as the college dorm example or maybe a weekly newspaper delivered to a small community. This is the most key idea about your market/message/media: you want them all as *specific* as possible! Most people do exactly the opposite. They say general messages to lots of people through vague and expensive medias.

With that in mind, this formula will determine the success of your marketing and communication:

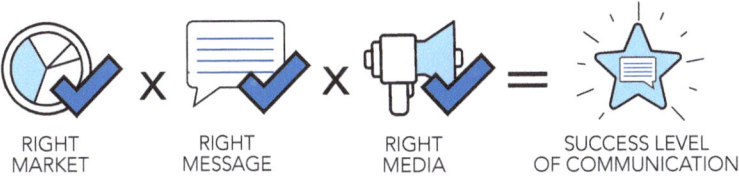

The above formula shows that if you say just the right thing, to the right people, but with a media type that they never see, you will have zero results. But if you can just tweak that media type and put the same message into a media type that your ideal market sees and hears, you may have a runaway success.

Now, I have an even better version of this already great concept. It's the Marketing Specificity Formula and takes into consideration the crucial *timing* of your marketing communications.

Your market is who you are communicating with, but also *when* in their life or journey you are communicating with them. For

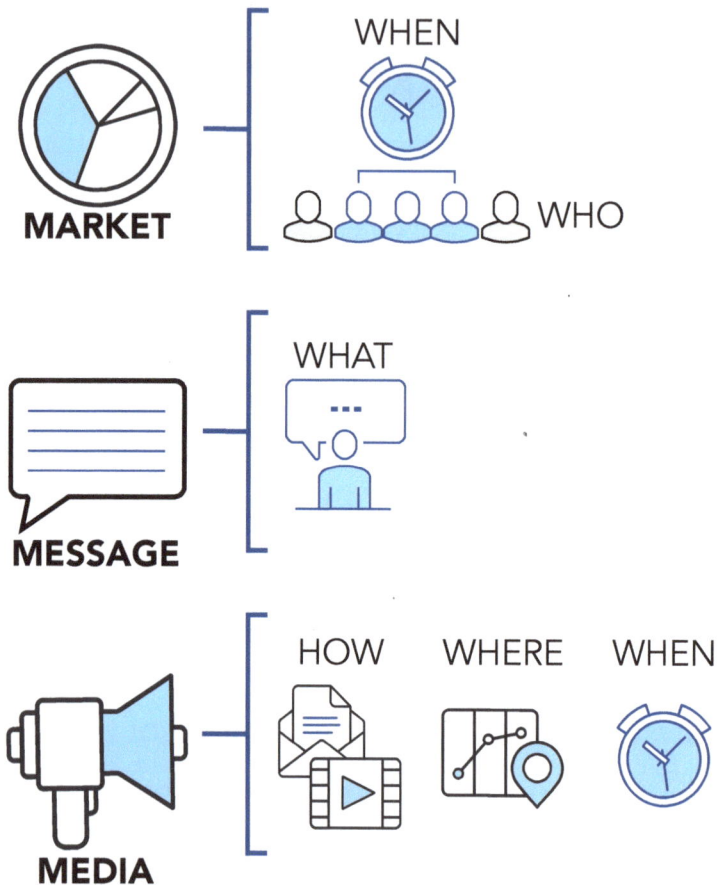

example, you may be marketing to male motorcycle riders. The "when" would be if they're just purchasing a motorcycle or if they have owned one for years. In a way, each "when" simply defines a more specific market (new bike owners vs. ones who have owned for years), but thinking in terms of "when" you are communicating to your market may help you better define the market.

Your message is what you are saying to your market. It's the headlines you use, the offers you make, etc.

And the media is "how" you are communicating, and more specifically, "where" and "when" this communication takes place. So your media may be a weekly newspaper that is placed for free in convenient stores on the first day of the month. Said another way, the "how" is a weekly newspaper, the "where" is in a convenient store, and the "when" is from the 1st of the month on until the papers are gone.

The point of the Marketing Specificity Formula is to get you to really drill down on who you are talking to, what are you saying, and through what means. Simple, but so important.

Now, look at your current "messages" and evaluate them according to the above analysis.

Take a few minutes and think about the markets, messages and medias you currently use. List out a few examples so you start to see how non-specific your messages may be.

THE MARKETING SPECIFICITY WORKSHEET

Who is the Audience	What is the Message	Through What Means

THE FOUR CLIENT TYPES

....

CHAPTER FIVE

....

So now you understand the basics of communicating with prospective clients. Before we go further let me discuss what I call the Four Client Types.

In the examples so far, we have been communicating with immediate prospective clients. These are clients who are ready to hire an attorney. And we really haven't discussed "how" we are trying to communicate with them other than to say what our communication to them was going to be.

But let me introduce a concept that may help give you some perspective on where this type of communication fits in the scheme of a complete practice.

There are really four types of 'clients' you can try to communicate with.

PROSPECTIVE

NEED HELP NOW AND
READY TO HIRE

CURRENT

CLIENTS YOU
CURRENTLY REPRESENT

FUTURE

MAY NEED HELP IN THE
FUTURE BUT NOT TODAY

FORMER

CLIENTS REPRESENTED
IN THE PAST

The first is the prospective client, one that is currently injured and ready to hire an attorney in the near future. He has a need for services soon. This is usually the type everyone wants to talk about and try to reach out to. Generally your communications to this person should focus on answering their immediate questions regarding their injury and future.

But, there's also *your* current client who you represent now. You do in fact communicate with them regularly. What are you saying to them?

There are also former clients who you previously helped. These 'clients' can also be communicated with by you and your law firm (indeed, these are arguably some of the best clients to stay in touch with, but that's a whole different discussion).

Finally, there is the fourth type of client, a 'future' client who is not yet hurt, is not currently looking for a lawyer, but may get hurt in the future and could be a great fit for you then.

And within each of these categories of clients, there are different ways you can (and should) communicate with them. For example, you may run a radio ad that is played one time and heard by a prospective client only once. This would be very 'temporary' media that comes and goes immediately. Or, you place an ad in the yellow pages. In this case, the prospective client may see the ad more than once. The ad is much more 'permanent.'

Finally, understand that "what" you're communicating also makes a difference. You may be communicating very helpful legal information and the law, such as the statute of limitations on their claim that they need to file soon. This would be a very relevant communication about their injury and should be primarily directed at current or prospective clients.

Or you may be providing less injury-relevant information, such an article in your law firm newsletter that discusses what you and your family did last summer. (Notice I did not say 'less relevant' here. Non-legal information plays an extremely important part in communicating with your future and former clients).

Assuming your messages are good, (which

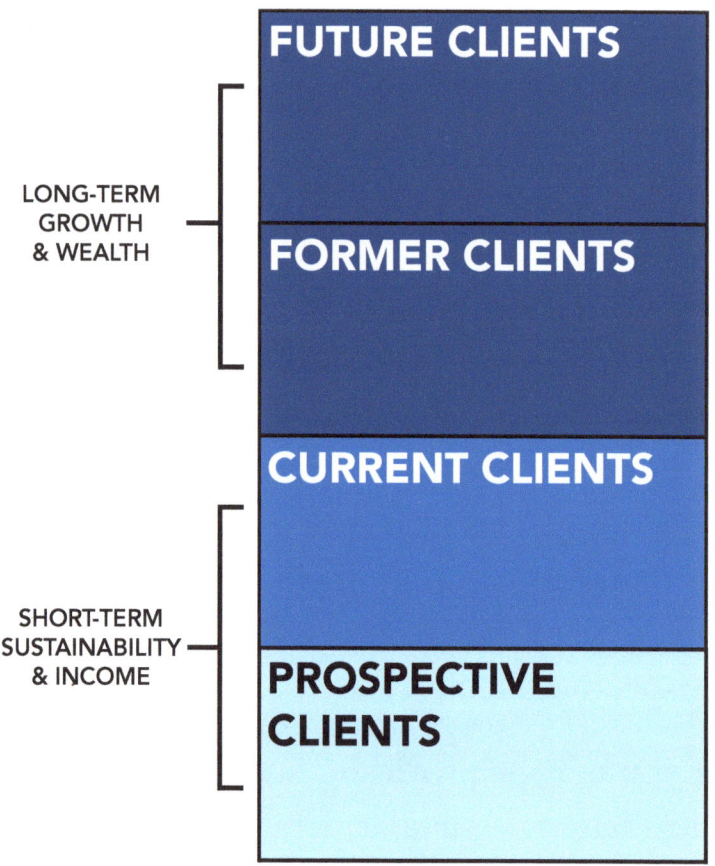

is a HUGE assumption and we will discuss this in the next chapter), then as you communicate with all four types of clients, you are building a stronger, more dependable practice. The more effort invested, the more profitable your practice will be in the long run.

Notice also that usually the foundation of the practice is the communications to immediate, prospective clients. Cash flow is important. At least *some* effort needs to be made at getting clients in the door now. And once your efforts at getting current clients is developed sufficiently, then you should work on creating strong communications for your former clients.

Finally, you should focus on reaching out to the community of people who may need you in the future. This builds a solid foundation of future clients. Now, if you are strong enough in communicating with your former clients or strong enough in communicating with your community of future clients, in theory you may not have to speak to those who are currently injured. Indeed, years ago many law firms did well simply through former client referrals. But today this usually doesn't work anymore for a variety of reasons. Now, let's figure out how to make a strong message.

HOW WILL THEY REMEMBER YOU?

....

CHAPTER SIX

....

Have you ever been to a car showroom to look at buying a new car? I don't mean a used car from a nice trusted lot where you buy all your cars. I mean a brand new, make-your-friends-jealous, drive off the showroom floor type car. The kind you greatly overpay for and the dealer makes a killing on.

What's the first thing they give you when you leave the lot if you tell then you 'have to think about it'? It's not their business card, that's for damn sure. And they don't let you leave empty handed if they're smart. They give you a big slick glossy color booklet with lots of pictures of your new car. Now why would they do this? Simple, it's basically a lead generator/converter for them. I call it a Value Gift. It has 'value' to the consumer, and it's a 'gift' given to you. That booklet stares at you for the next 5 days and you see those slick pictures of your dream car. It's a little piece of the dealership showroom following you home, sitting on your table and entering the conversation in your head each day trying to convert you into a new car buyer.

So, when a possible client comes to your website, what are you 'giving' them? Probably nothing, like 99% of the law firms across the country. Ok, but when they call you and talk to you for 30 minutes and tell you they 'will think about it', what do you send to them after the call? Still nothing?

Alright, let's say they take the time to come to 'your showroom' (your office). They ask lots of questions and seem interested, but need to 'think about it' or maybe 'talk it over with their spouse'. Or worse, they have to visit some other 'showrooms' before making a decision. Well, for these people, what do you give them to take home so they can remember you and bring a little piece of you home with them? Your business card?

Seriously?

And if you are thinking right now, 'gee, I'm not selling cars and my clients should be happy to hire me without me having to sell myself' then you are living in 1954 when being a lawyer was a rare thing. Nowadays, we aren't rare at all, so you have to have some means to 'continue' the conversation with a possible client long after the leave your website or your office.

For consumers looking for legal services, a Value Gift serves another tremendously important purpose: it allows for a scared, hesitant, non-trusting possible client to raise their hand ever so slightly without fear of getting it chopped off by you. It's a 'warm and easy' way for a possible client to start the hiring dance with you. Compare that to the alternative of either calling a 'LAW FIRM' (big, bad, scary place) or, gulp, physically going to a law firm to meet in person with a LAWYER (scary person who just wants money from me). The simple point is that some sort of a Value Gift [deliverable/lead generator/lead magnet/lead converter] helps grease the skids for your clients to come to you. It serves as one of the first communications you have with a potential client and this is a fantastic opportunity! It let's you craft how they will see you. First impressions matter.

FINAL THOUGHTS AND MOVING FORWARD

CHAPTER SEVEN

This short booklet is meant to start the wheels turning in your head. The concepts here are pretty basic to understand, but can take years to implement and master. Many people know "how" to play golf or other sports, yet they practice and take lessons again and again. Creating strong, valuable communications for your legal clients that get them to run to your office for help is much the same thing. It's an ongoing process checking each step of the process and tightening any holes that cause the communication to fall flat. **The only thing worse than not spending money and investing in your practice, is spending money on communications and methods that don't work.**

It's time to get serious about growing your

law practice. I created the two-year Thriving Practices program to teach good, smart lawyers how to create successful practices. Having control over your practice to intentionally grow it is an amazing feeling! Invest in a continuous asset that ensures years and years of future income and quality of time for you.

ABOUT THE AUTHOR

TIMOTHY YOUNG

Tim Young has practiced law for more than 23 years and runs his own highly successful practice of 4 attorneys with 13 employees. He has studied the best marketing and ways to communicate with clients for years

and has been coached by and consulted with the top experts in multiple fields including copy-writing, business growth, marketing and personal coaching.

He lives in New Orleans with his wife and two children, George (age 20) and Julia (age

16). He's a constant learner.

You can get more information about his transformative Thriving Practices programs at www.TheThrivingPractices.com.

www.ingramcontent.com/pod-product-compliance
Lightning Source LLC
Chambersburg PA
CBHW040815200526
45159CB00024B/2979